LINCOLN'S GETTYSBURG ADDRESS

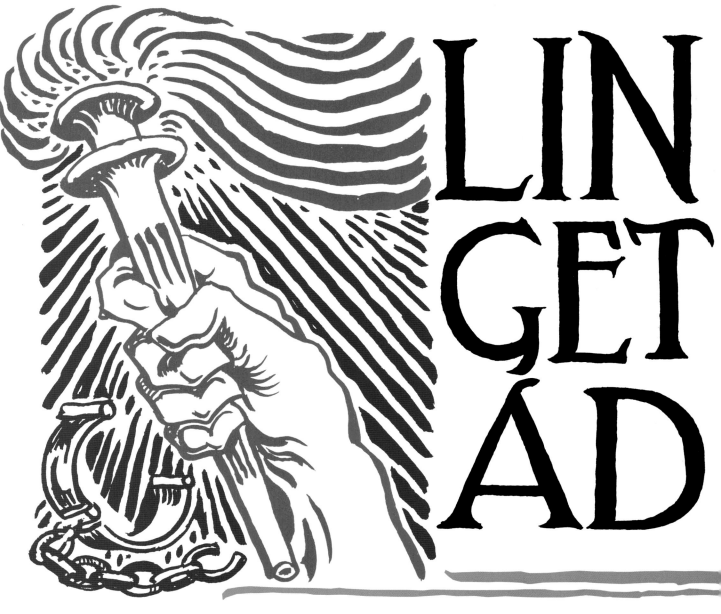

LIN
GET
AD

A PICTORIAL
PAINTED BY

ALBERT WHITMAN+CO

COLN'S TYSBURG DRESS

IN TERPRETATION JAMES DAUGHERTY

PUBLISHERS · CHICAGO

Library of Congress Cataloging-in-Publication Data

Daugherty, James Henry.
Lincoln's Gettysburg address : a pictorial interpretation painted by James Daugherty.
p. cm.
Originally published: 1947. With a new afterword by Gabor Boritt.
ISBN 978-0-8075-4550-8
I. Boritt, G. S. II. Lincoln, Abraham. Gettysburg address. III. Title.
ND237.D27A5 2013
759.13—dc23
2012013288

For more information about Albert Whitman & Company,
please visit our web site at www.albertwhitman.com

FOREWORD

After the solemn prayer and two hours of Edward Everett's classic oratory composed for the occasion, Lincoln slowly rose, drew from his pocket two sheets of paper, and delivered the Gettysburg Address. He spoke for about two minutes. His ten sentences sounded native, direct, and clear after Everett's long, formal oratory.

"Lamon, this is a flat failure and the people are disappointed," Lincoln said gloomily to a friend after the ceremony, referring to his speech.

In happier mood the following day, he wrote in reply to Edward Everett's note of congratulation, "I am pleased to know that in your judgment the little I did say was not altogether a failure." Everett had written with fine sincerity and perception, "I should be glad if I could flatter myself that I came as near the central idea of the occasion in two hours as you did in two minutes."

The central idea—that was it. The thing that Lincoln could see and hold to through the red mists of war and the confusions of a dark and tragic time.

So much for the event—its time, scene, and actors.

Eighty years and more have passed since Lincoln spoke so briefly under a gray November sky in 1863, standing beside the newly buried dead on that field of bitter victory. His words have become a lasting testament of sorrow and dedication for all battlefields.

For us today Gettysburg is not only the consecrated Pennsylvania acres. It is the sacred soil of torn Pacific islands where the white crosses stand in rows; the hills of North Africa; the beach-heads of Italy and France; the blasted mountain ridges taken and retaken; the skeleton cities won house by house; the battlefields of the deep sky and the strewn sea bottom. Gettysburg means all these, and more.

Again we have stood at the close of a great war, the most terrible in history, with the unfinished task before us. At a time when events, directions, and purposes seem confused and the path ahead clouded and obscure, Lincoln's words are clear, strong, comforting, eloquent of the central idea. The stupendous rush of history has not ignored, but expanded and enriched their deepest meanings.

Because we are the sons of many peoples, races, and nations fused into spiritual oneness by the frightful bloodletting of two world wars, America has been called to and anointed for spiritual leadership of the world in the great task ahead.

Our government in its framework is an inseparable union of forty-eight free and independent though not sovereign states, bound together in mutual consent; and a union one and indivisible. Because this is so, America today stands and shows forth not merely as a possible theory or blueprint; but a tested working example for world federation, pointing the way to permanent world peace that is not a mere truce between wars. It is significant that the three departments of the United Nations Charter correspond functionally to the three fundamental branches—legislative, executive, and judicial—of our great Constitution.

We pause and look back on the long road to freedom, or at the stretch we have come from Plymouth Rock to Pearl Harbor. In spite of the failures and the betrayals, the long delays and setbacks, we the people have not failed. Our voice has spoken out clear and strong the testament of liberty. We know the names—Roger Williams, Washington, Franklin, Paine, Jefferson, Whitman, Lincoln, Wilson, Roosevelt, Willkie. These are only a few in the long roll call that have "sounded forth the trumpet that shall never call retreat."

Coming out of the native rank and file of America, Lincoln emerges as the archetype of democracy holding fast in darkest hour to the central idea—the Union—for if the Union fail, then democracy has failed.

After the blasts of wars, above the troubled clamor of uncertain peace, we are listening again to the voice of Gettysburg across the years. We hear the surging answer of the spirit of the people young and sure and strong: "We, the People of the United States, the American People, a new nation and race welded out of many peoples, faiths, hopes, tongues—we will keep our rendezvous with destiny. We will be there. We shall not fail."

James Daugherty

Weston
Connecticut

Lincoln's Gettysburg Address

Four score and seven years ago our fathers brought forth on this continent a new nation, conceived in Liberty, and dedicated to the proposition that all men are created equal.

Now we are engaged in a great civil war, testing whether that nation, or any nation so conceived and so dedicated, can long endure.

We are met on a great battlefield of that war. We have come to dedicate a portion of that field as a final resting place for those who here gave their lives that that nation might live. It is altogether fitting and proper that we should do this. But, in a larger sense, we can not dedicate—we can not consecrate—we can not hallow—this ground. The brave men, living and dead, who struggled here, have consecrated it far above our poor power to add or detract. The world will little note nor long remember what we say here, but it can never forget what they did here. It is for us, the living, rather, to be dedicated here to the unfinished work which they who fought here have thus far so nobly advanced. It is rather for us to be here dedicated to the great task remaining before us—that from these honored dead we take increased devotion to that cause for which they gave the last full measure of devotion—that we here highly resolve that these dead shall not have died in vain—that this nation, under God, shall have a new birth of freedom—and that government of the people, by the people, for the people, shall not perish from the earth.

Abraham Lincoln

Gettysburg, *November 19, 1863*

FOUR SCORE AND
OUR FATHERS BROUGHT

SEVEN YEARS AGO
FORTH ON THIS CONTINENT

A NEW NATION CON

CEIVED IN LIBERTY

AND DEDICATED TO
THAT ALL MEN ARE

THE PROPOSITION
CREATED EQUAL

NOW WE ARE ENGAGED IN A
TESTING WHETHER THAT
CONCEIVED AND SO DEDI

WE ARE MET
OF THAT WAR WE HAVE COME
OF THAT FIELD AS A

ON A GREAT BATTLEFIELD
TO DEDICATE A PORTION
FINAL RESTING PLACE

for THOSE WHO
THEIR LIVES
MIGHT LIVE
FITTING AND
WE SHOULD

HERE GAVE
THAT THAT NATION
IT IS ALTOGETHER
PROPER THAT
DO THIS

GER SENSE
DEDICATE
CONSECRATE
HALLOW
GROUND

THE BRAVE MEN DEAD WHO HERE HAVE IT FAR ABOVE POWER TO ADD

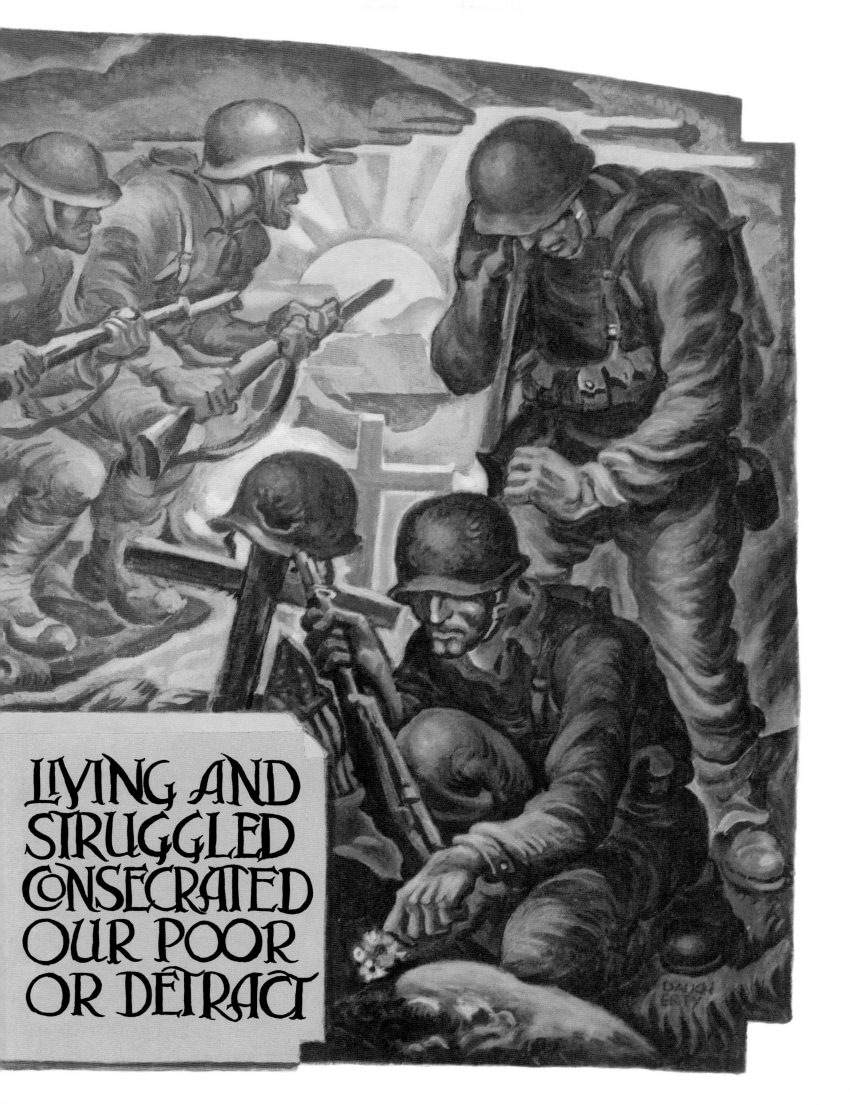

LIVING AND
STRUGGLED
CONSECRATED
OUR POOR
OR DETRACT

THE WORLD
NOR LONG
WHAT WE
BUT IT CAN
WHAT THEY

IT IS FOR US
RATHER TO BE
HERE TO THE
WORK WHICH
FOUGHT HERE
SO NOBLY

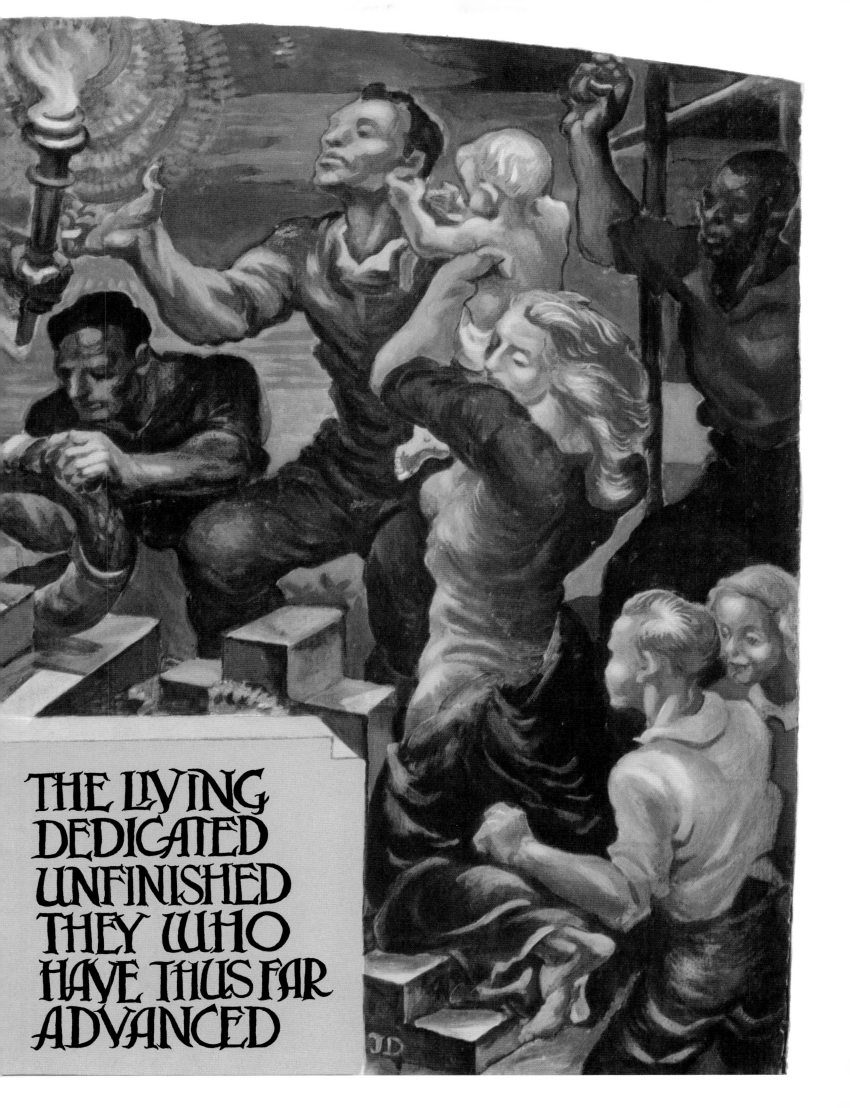

THE LIVING
DEDICATED
UNFINISHED
THEY WHO
HAVE THUS FAR
ADVANCED

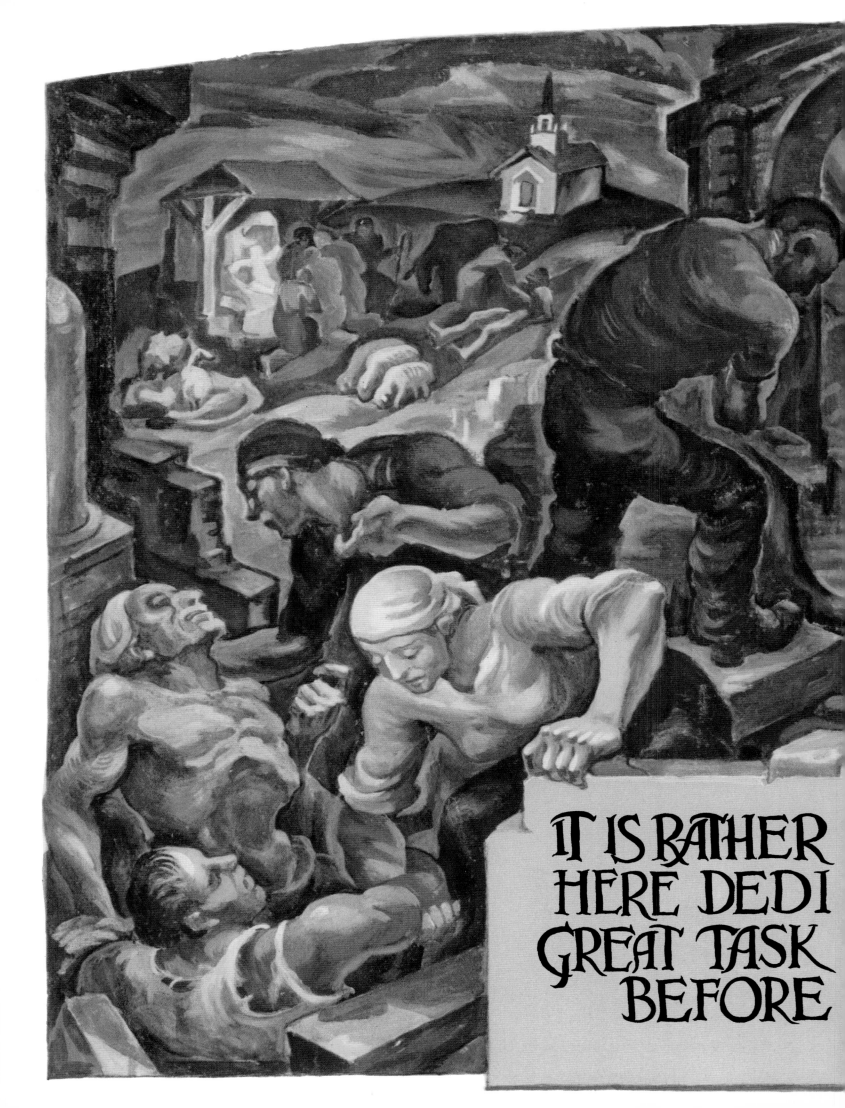

FOR US TO BE
GATED TO THE
REMAINING
US

THAT FROM THESE
WE TAKE INCREAS
TO THAT CAUSE
GAVE THE
MEASURE of

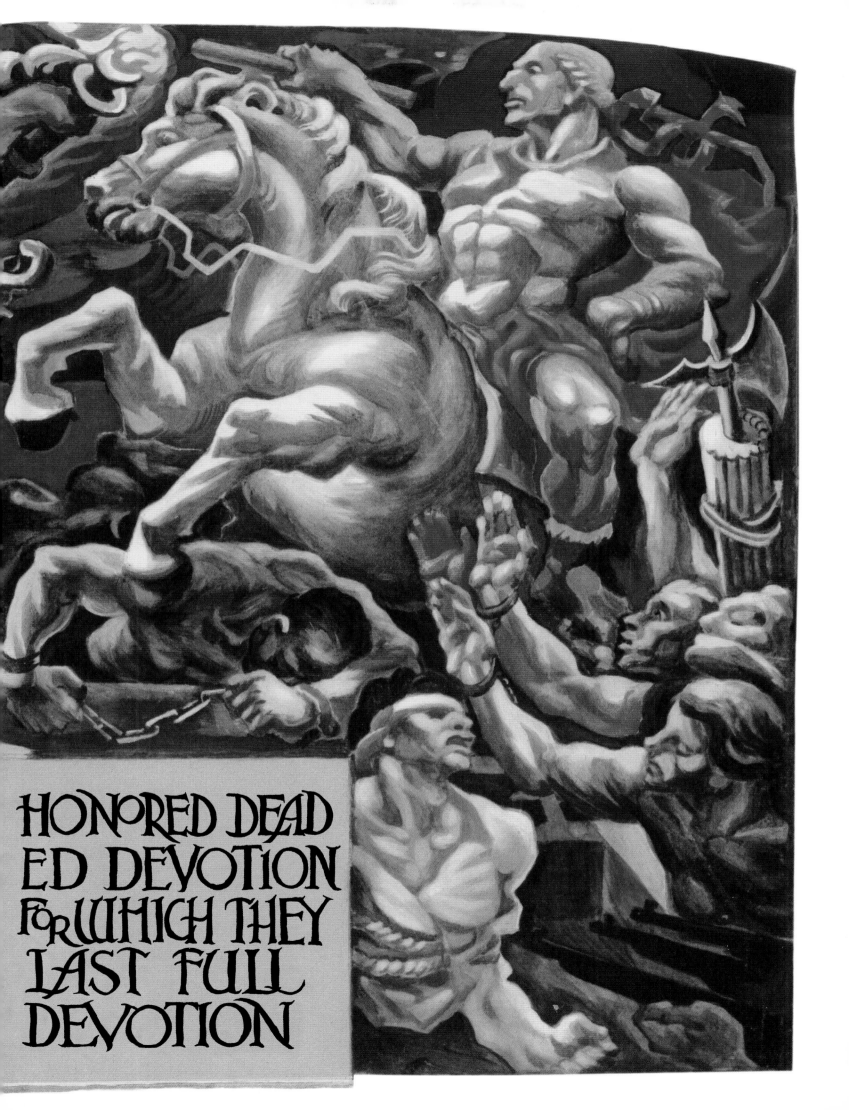

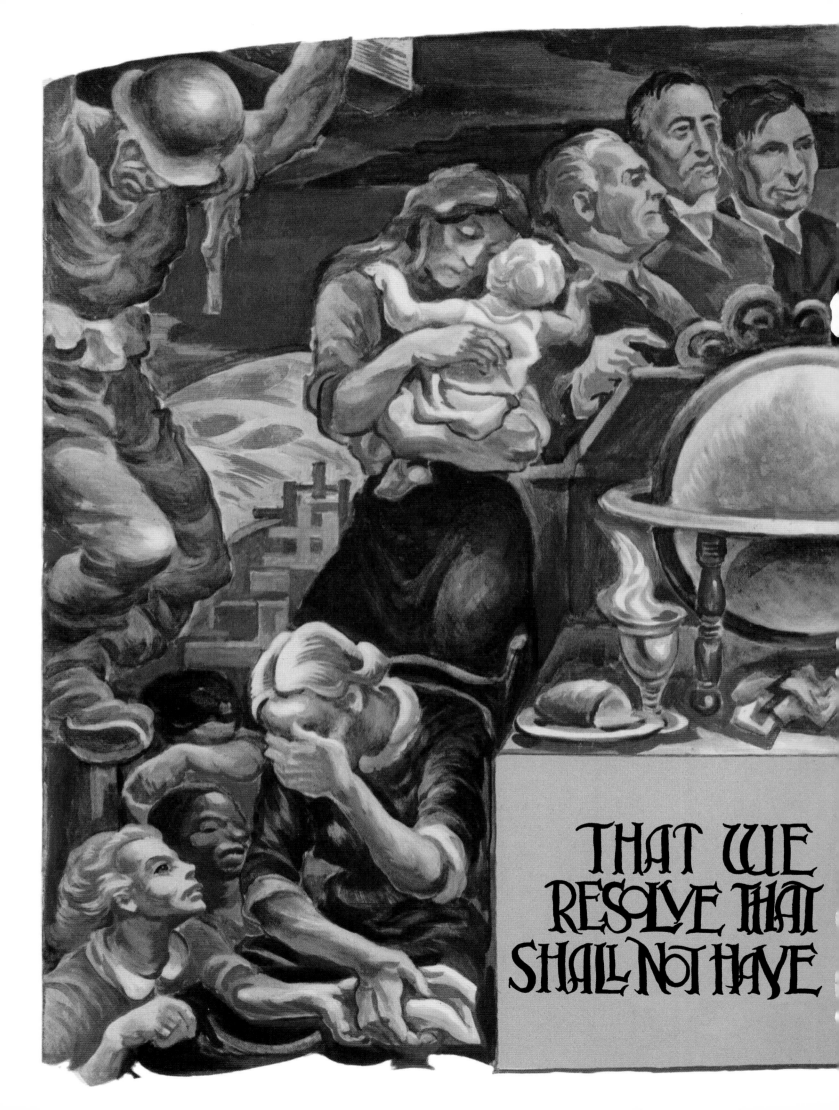

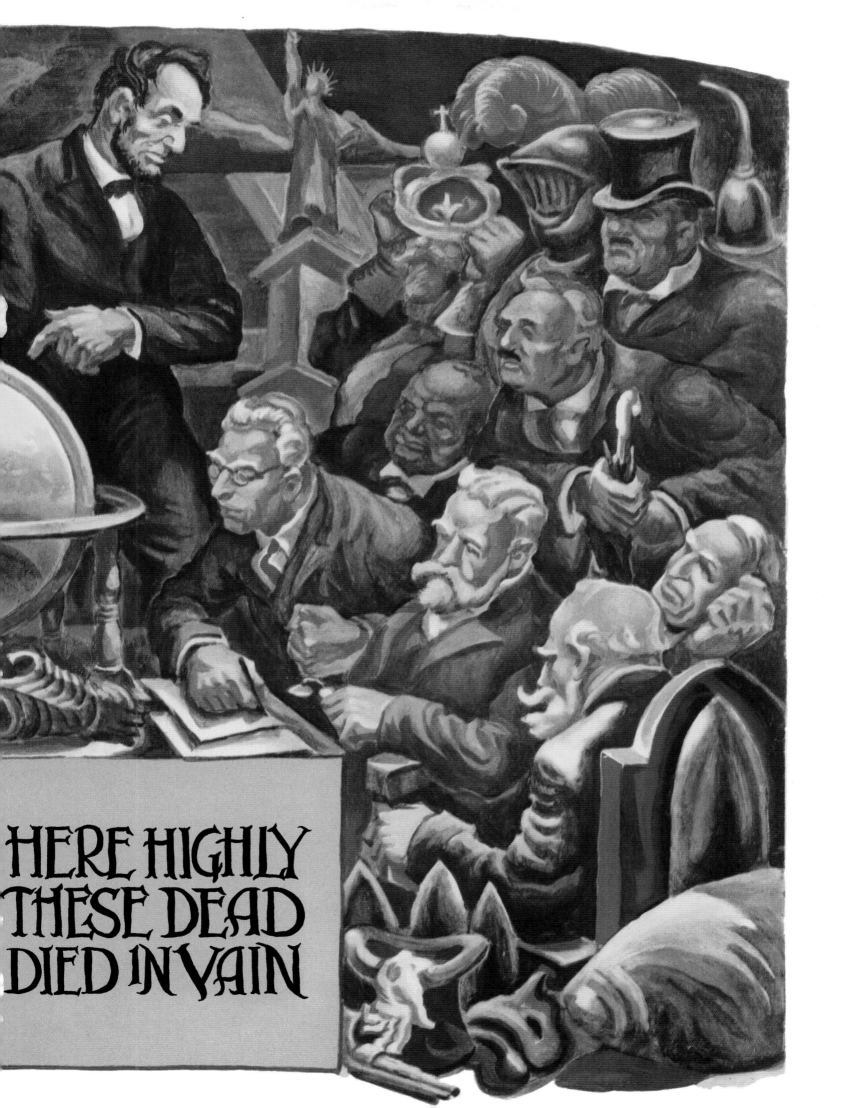

HERE HIGHLY
THESE DEAD
DIED IN VAIN

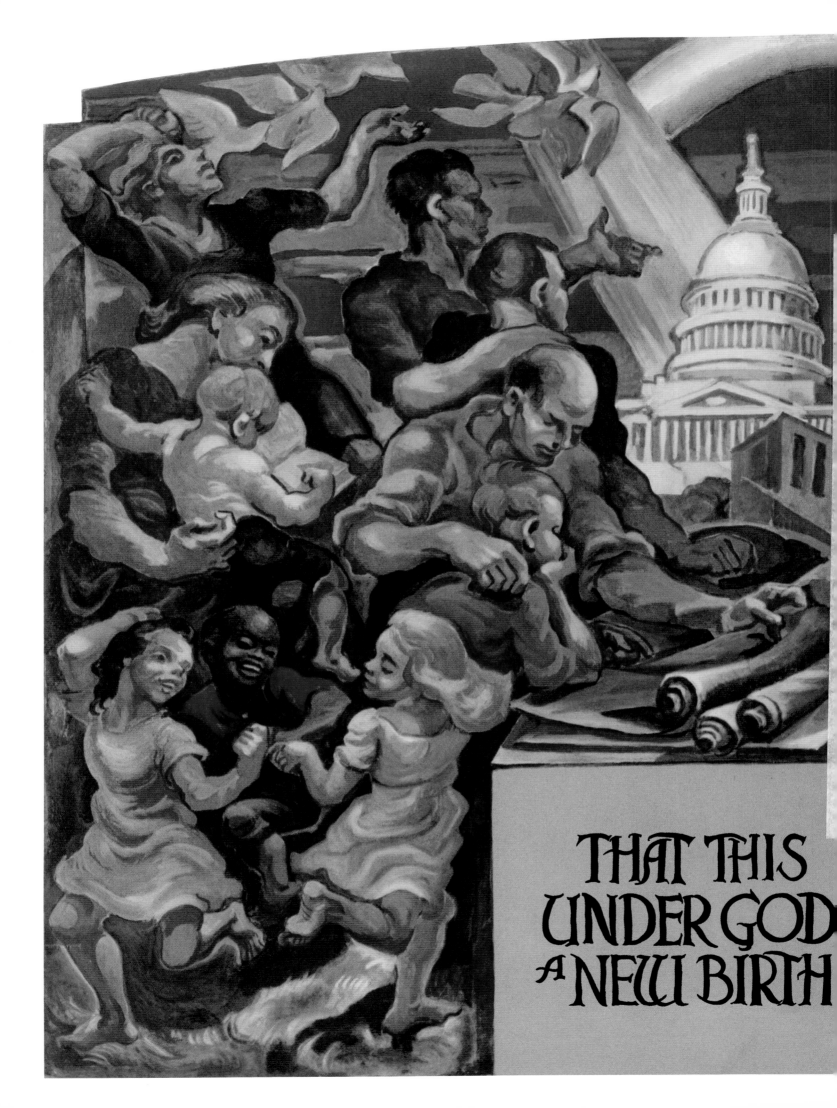

THAT THIS
UNDER GOD
A NEW BIRTH

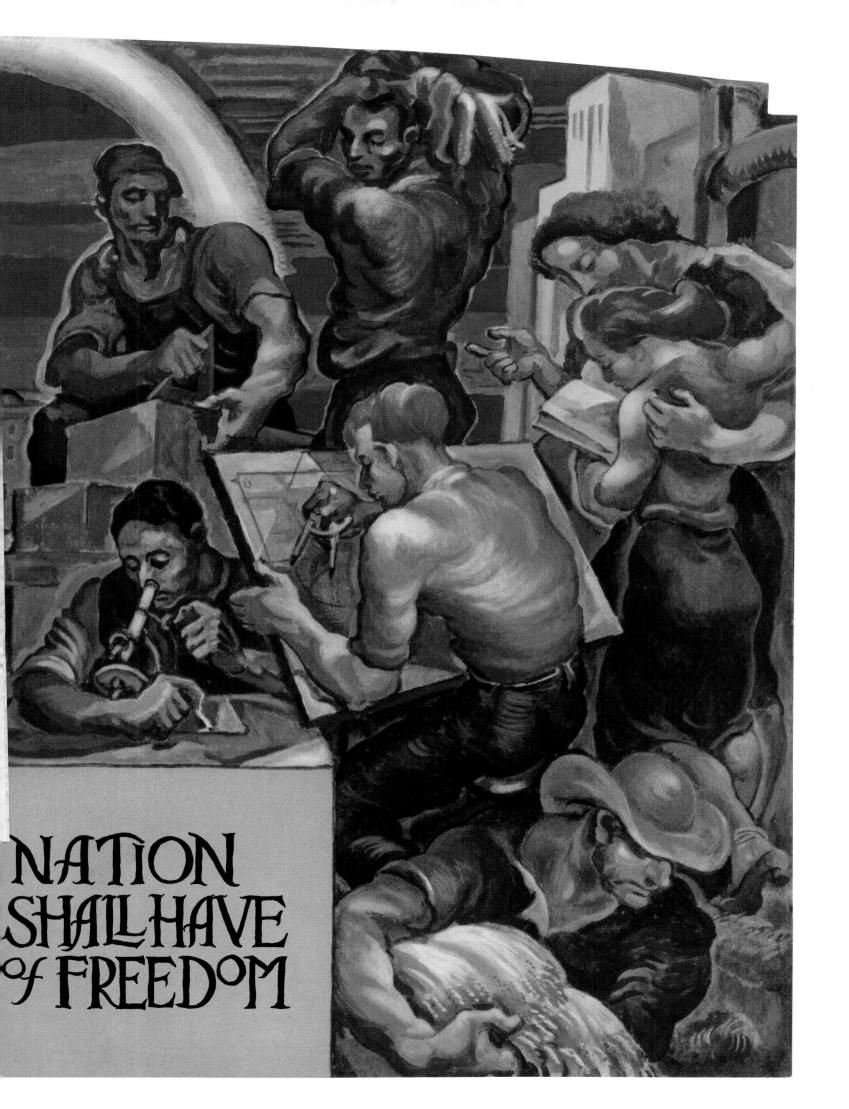

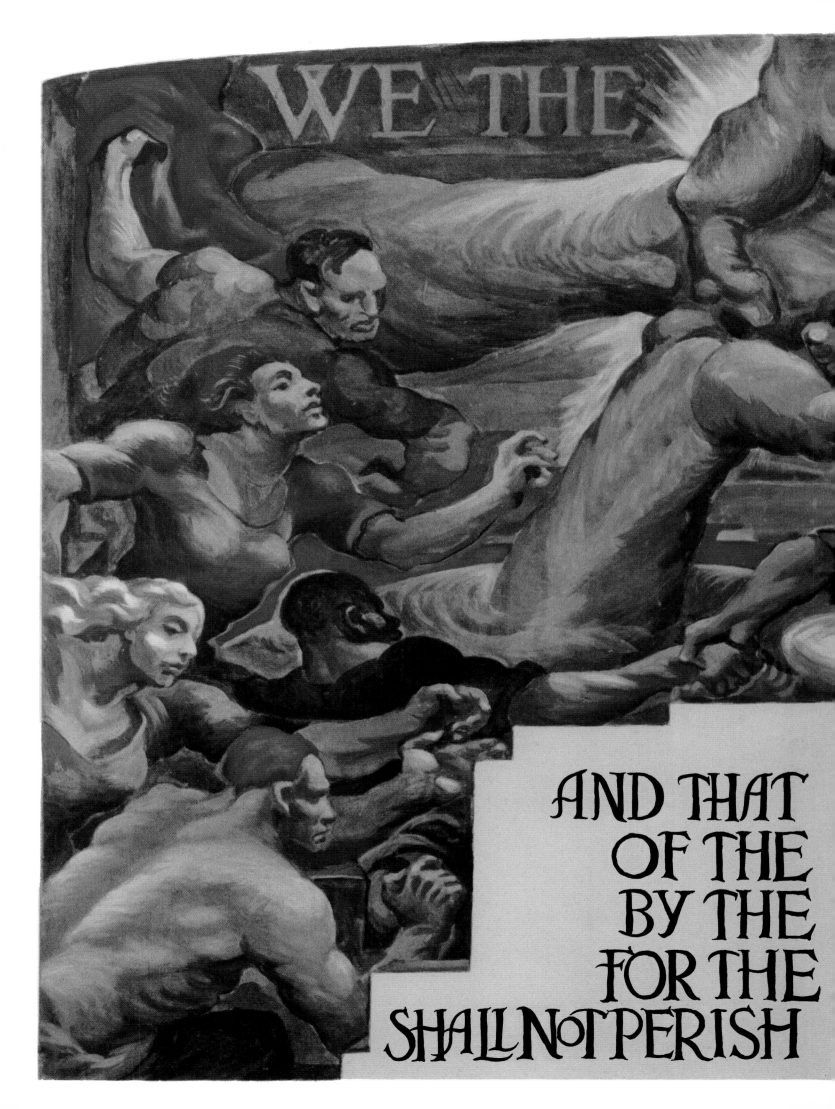

Correct Intellectual level

Olga Feliciano [felician@chipublib.org]
Sent: Monday, February 10, 2014 12:19 PM
To: @Carl User List

To: Conversion Liaisons

The correct intellectual level for *Lincoln's Gettysburg address : a pictorial interpretation painted by James Daugherty.* (bid # 8700268) is **ELEM.** The only thing that you have to do is change the spine label(s).
Below, you will find a copy of the items in the record before the changes:

Branch	Location	Call Number	Item Number	Status
AIRVNG	CEARLY	ND237.D27A5 2013	R0440479803	On Shelf
ARCHER	CEARLY	ND237.D27A5 2013	R0440491392	On Shelf
ATGELD	CEARLY	ND237.D27A5 2013	R0440490809	On Shelf
AUSTIN	CEARLY	ND237.D27A5 2013	R0440491960	On Shelf
AVALON	CEARLY	ND237.D27A5 2013	R0440492550	On Shelf
BACKOF	CEARLY	ND237.D27A5 2013	R0440493124	On Shelf
BEVERL	CEARLY	ND237.D27A5 2013	R0440494544	On Shelf
BLKSTN	CEARLY	ND237.D27A5 2013	R0440468022	Charged
BUDLON	CEARLY	ND237.D27A5 2013	R0440478271	On Shelf
BZAZIN	CEARLY	ND237.D27A5 2013	R0440495249	On Shelf
COLEMA	CEARLY	ND237.D27A5 2013	R0440489010	On Shelf
DUNN	CEARLY	ND237.D27A5 2013	R0440485749	On Shelf
GGRAND	CEARLY	ND237.D27A5 2013	R0440486452	On Shelf
HOWLC	C2EARL	ND237.D27A5 2013	R0440480600	On Shelf
HEGEWI	CEARLY	ND237.D27A5 2013	R0440489557	On Shelf
LVILL	CEARLY	ND237.D27A5 2013	R0440486981	On Shelf
MTGRWD	CEARLY	ND237.D27A5 2013	R0440490176	On Shelf
RMD	CEARLY	ND237.D27A5 2013	R0440487602	On Shelf
UPTOWN	CEARLY	ND237.D27A5 2013	R0440488399	On Shelf
WCHGO	CEARLY	ND237.D27A5 2013	R0440483543	On Shelf
WPULLM	CEARLY	ND237.D27A5 2013	R0440484214	On Shelf
WTOWN	CEARLY	ND237.D27A5 2013	R0440485024	On Shelf
WWOOD	CEARLY	ND237.D27A5 2013	R0440479065	On Shelf

Thank you,

Olga Feliciano
Head, Database Maintenance Unit
Chicago Public Library
Catalog Unit
400 S. State Street, Rm. 3S-12,
Chicago, IL 60605
Phone number: (312) 747-4651
Catalog Unit phone number: (312) 747-4660

ABRAHAM LINCOLN DID NOT KNOW THAT HE WOULD BE DELIVERING THE GETTYSBURG ADDRESS ON NOVEMBER 19, 1863, UNTIL A FEW DAYS BEFOREHAND.

To be the president of the United States was overwhelming, especially during the Civil War. (Even in the twenty-first century, the presidency is, at times, bewildering—and also wonderful.) For the dedication of the National Cemetery in Gettysburg, William Seward did come prepared with a speech. He became the president's closest friend and one of the best-known secretaries of state—he later became known for buying Alaska. Seward understood that Lincoln was a one-of-a-kind individual. And they both believed that the people could save the United States of America.

Seward wrote his speech for his own "Gettysburg Address" ahead of time. He gave it the night before Lincoln's in Gettysburg, in a building right next to the Wills House, where Lincoln stayed overnight, as did dozens of others. It was a celebration for many the whole night. In the end, when he gave his speech, the secretary of state made it clear that slavery was the central event of the war, and that Abraham Lincoln understood that.

The president himself came to Gettysburg on November 18—as did so many more, including Seward. Lincoln left the White House at noon. The train flew at 25 mph—an amazing pace for that time. They got to the Gettysburg station at dusk, and an immense crowd cheered him. He and the dignitaries walked the short distance to the Wills House, next to the town's center.

Today it is called the Lincoln Square. Then dinner came. It was repeatedly interrupted by boisterous masses, military bands, and a singing group. Loud voices called out, "Old Abe!" and "Father Abraham!" At last, Lincoln obliged to go outdoors.

"I do not appear before you for the purpose of speechifying," he said; he had "several substantial reasons. The most substantial of these is that I have no speech to make." The crowd laughed. People expected Abe to be funny; they liked what they were getting. "It is somewhat important in my position that one should not say any foolish things if he can help it . . ."

"*If* you can help it," a voice rang out. The delighted crowd laughed again heartily.

" . . . and to help it is to say nothing at all. Believing that that is my precise position this evening, I must beg you from saying one word."

In 118 or so words, Lincoln acquitted himself: his first Gettysburg "address." The next day the main speaker would be Edward Everett.

We should remember that Everett was the most distinguished orator at the time: a New England minister, professor, Harvard president, governor of Massachusetts, congressman, senator, secretary of state, and presidential candidate in 1860. But he did not support Abraham Lincoln because there were four candidates at that time, and Everett was in some ways conservative. By November 1863, he was ready to support the president.

Most people today think that orators are rather boring. In those days, however, speeches were central to political life—it was considered entertainment in an era before television, modern sports, Internet, phones, and more. So Everett spoke for two hours, extemporaneously, in spite of the fact that he was seventy years old and had had a stroke. Some said it was his best speech ever. He spoke about the battle at great length, but in the most important part of the oration, he spoke about countries who fought each other over long periods of time but in the end made peace among themselves. That's what Everett hoped for: peace after the Civil War.

After Everett, and before we get back to Lincoln's address, we need to pause. We need to talk a little about the artist and his work, which is not only about the Gettysburg Address but also about the second World War. The two wars are connected. One of the most respected American historians of the last fifty years, Arthur Schlesinger Jr. explained boldly that the American republic "has gone through two awful times of testing since the achievement of independence—two times when the life of the nation was critically at stake . . ." The two presidents were Lincoln and Franklin D. Roosevelt.

Lincoln's Gettysburg Address was created by James Daugherty (1889, Ashville–1974, Boston), who wrote this book two years after the second World War. He was a painter and illustrator. One of his children's works won the Newbery Award, and another was nominated for the Caldecott Award. Not surprisingly his Gettysburg Address colors are bright and bold; adults and children can enjoy them equally.

The book begins with the early Puritans and Thomas Jefferson, George Washington, Benjamin Franklin, and ends after the second World War. His people are women, men, and children; black, brown, blond, and Asian. We haven't seen a Gettysburg Address book like this since. The artist was a special man.

Then the address. The solemn tone changed totally in the morning by the people. Consecration.

Lincoln finished part of his text in the White House—the rest, that night in Gettysburg. The full second version was completed late that night or in the morning, though we cannot be entirely certain. Later there would be three revisions, but the most important change he made at the cemetery on the morning of the nineteenth: "under God."

Earlier in the morning, Lincoln went on a battlefield tour with Seward, and he came back to the Wills House. Then the people and Lincoln were ready to go. He got on his horse and his text was with him.

Funeral music. The cemetery. Respected silence for the president. Men and women were supposed to be separated, but the sexes were mixed together by the crowds. Then the music stopped. A Methodist minister stood up and gave a very long prayer. The ending finished with the Lord's Prayer, and the multitudes joined spontaneously. Yet the president's young secretary, John Hay, commented irreverently in his diary: The preacher made "a prayer which thought it was an oration." Lincoln's speech was four times shorter.

But then perhaps the most beautiful hymn followed: "The Old Hundred." Next, Edward Everett. Two hours. Applause. Next, a consecration chant: "This is holy ground." Lincoln would follow briefly. There would be a dirge and a short benediction. Amen.

"Four score and seven years ago"—Abraham Lincoln's Gettysburg Address. He reminded people of the Declaration of Independence of July 4, 1776. "Liberty . . . All men are created equal. . . War. . . Great battlefield . . . The living and dead." The future. Lincoln spoke to the world. We are the people. This is who we are. "That this nation, under God, shall have a new birth of freedom—and that government of the people, by the people, for the people, shall not perish from the earth."

— *Gabor Boritt, Emeritus*
Civil War Institute
Fluhrer Professor of Civil War Studies
Gettysburg College

This afterword is dedicated to PAUL R. S. BORITT. He saved the lives of thousands of people at the end of the second World War in Hungary.

Address delivered at the dedication of the cemetery at Gettysburg.

Four score and seven years ago our fathers brought forth on this continent, a new nation, conceived in Liberty, and dedicated to the proposition that all men are created equal.

Now we are engaged in a great civil war, testing whether that nation, or any nation so conceived and so dedicated, can long endure. We are met on a great battle field of that war. We have come to dedicate a portion of that field, as a final resting place for those who here gave their lives, that that nation might live. It is altogether fitting and proper that we should do this.

But, in a larger sense, we can not dedicate — we can not consecrate — we can not hallow — this ground. The brave men, living and dead, who struggled here have consecrated it, far above our poor power to add or detract. The world will little note, nor long remember what we say here, but it can never forget what they did here. It is for us the living, rather, to be dedicated here to the unfinished work which they who fought here have thus far so nobly advanced. It is rather for us to be here dedicated to the great task remaining before us — that from these honored dead we take increased devotion to that cause for which they gave the last full measure of devotion — that we here highly resolve that these dead shall not have died in vain — that this nation, under God, shall have a new birth of freedom — and that government of the people, by the people, for the people, shall not perish from the earth.

Abraham Lincoln.

By permission of Mrs. William J. A. Bliss and Miss Eleanor A. Bliss, Baltimore, Md.

November 19. 1863.

James Daugherty's interpretations of his paintings for

Lincoln's Gettysburg Address

Painting Number One

Four score and seven years ago our fathers brought forth on this continent . . .

Lincoln here refers to the founding fathers of 1776. They are depicted in the right-hand group. Jefferson is reading the Declaration of Independence. Below him sits Benjamin Franklin, and beside him Tom Paine inscribes COMMON SENSE on a drumhead. Behind Paine stands a patriot of the people's army.

Against the flag is Washington, beside him Samuel Adams. On the left the Pilgrim Father with the Bible and the Pilgrim Woman, kneeling on Plymouth Rock, typify the spiritual aspiration of democracy. The young axman below and the soldier, Miles Standish, signify the physical conquest of the wilderness. In the background the rainbow of promise shines over the storm clouds.

Painting Number Two

. . . a new nation conceived in liberty . . .

On the right, the group signifies the integrity of the family as the basic social unit of our national life. The figure on the left is unshackling a slave. Two figures are raising our flag on the cornerstone of the Constitution. In the sky the eagle of Freedom is mounting toward the rising sun of enlightenment.

AND DEDICATED TO THE PROPOSITION
THAT ALL MEN ARE CREATED EQUAL

NOW WE ARE ENGAGED IN A GREAT CIVIL WAR
TESTING WHETHER THAT NATION OR ANY NATION SO
CONCEIVED AND SO DEDI CATED CAN LONG ENDURE

Painting Number Three

. . . and dedicated to the proposition that all men are created equal . . .

This scene depicts the beginning of the westward march and the equality of opportunity afforded by the vast westward frontiers. The ox-drawn blue Conestoga wagons wind over the Wilderness Road to Kentucky. The buckskin backwoodsman in the foreground is of course Daniel Boone. Behind him, a young settler and his bride are riding off to build a home on the frontier.

Painting Number Four

Now we are engaged in a great Civil War, testing whether that nation, or any nation so conceived and so dedicated can long endure . . .

This design depicts the House Divided. In the right foreground is the fanatic, John Brown; beside him, Harriet Beecher Stowe. Above is the figure of Lincoln whose head is bowed with the tragedy of civil war. Beside him are Sherman and Grant on one side, and Stanton and Seward on the other. Beneath is Walt Whitman, and a young Union soldier taking farewell of his sweetheart. In the background, the unfinished dome of the Capitol looms against the drab clouds of war.

On the left, Lee sits on his horse, Traveller. Beside him are Stonewall Jackson and J. E. B. Stuart. A cheering rebel soldier waves the Confederate flag. Below, slaves are picking cotton; and in the background is the portico of a southern mansion, a symbol of the plantation aristocracy.

Painting Number Five

We are met on a great battlefield of that war. We have come to dedicate a portion of that field as a final resting place . . .

This is of course an imaginative conception and not a realistic view of Lincoln delivering his Address.

Painting Number Six

. . . for those who here gave their lives that that nation might live. It is altogether fitting and proper that we should do this . . .

Figures stand with bowed heads, and kneel, in memory of the dead of all wars. In the background, rays of sunlight break through clouds. This panel is intended to express a mood rather than an actual scene.

Painting Number Seven

But in a larger sense we cannot dedicate, we cannot consecrate, we cannot hallow this ground . . .

The group of young people on the right look forward to the future with courage and hope. The pioneers of the Oregon Trail look up in faith as they enter the vast reaches of the westward landscape.

Painting Number Eight

The brave men living and dead who struggled here have consecrated it far above our poor power to add or detract . . .

Lincoln's words apply to all who have sacrificed for liberty on every battlefield. On the left is the Concord patriot, the minuteman of the Revolution. On the right, soldiers of World War II place flowers on the graves of comrades fallen on battlefields all over the world. Across the center moves a procession of the soldiers who have fought for freedom throughout our history.

Painting Number Nine

The world will little note nor long remember what we say here. But it can never forget what they did here . . .

On the right, the plow and the rising corn succeed the devastation of war. On the left, Lincoln meditates against a sunset sky in which a vision of marching armies moves in cloud shapes.

Painting Number Ten

It is for us the living rather to be dedicated here to the unfinished work which they who fought here have thus far so nobly advanced . . .

At the Tomb of the Unknown Soldier the spirits of our heroic dead pass on the torch of freedom to succeeding generations.

Painting Number Eleven

It is rather for us to be here dedicated to the great task remaining before us . . .

On the left, the task of restoring a war-shattered world is suggested by the women ministering to the destitute among the ruins of a European city. Behind them is a vision of the Nativity and of the Good Samaritan, suggesting the spirit of Christianity and of compassion as the motives in building a democratic world.

In the right foreground a Union and a Confederate soldier clasp hands as a symbol of our united nation. Behind them a slave is awakening to freedom. In the center, workers are laying the foundations of a united nation. An emancipated woman, dressed in red, points to a vision of a new America rising in the future.

Painting Number Twelve

That from these honored dead we take increased devotion to that cause for which they gave the last full measure of devotion . . .

At the center left, the figure of Freedom advances, holding the torch of Liberty and the scales of Justice. She is treading on the serpent of lying propaganda which tries to poison the democratic spirit. Below her, Jefferson, holding the Bill of Rights, points to crosses of the honored dead. Directly behind him an old man is imparting the democratic traditions to a child. In the background is the citizen soldier ready for defense.

On the right, the totalitarian dictator rides over his shackled people. Below, his red-handed followers raise their chained hands in the Fascist salute, while a blindfolded liberal faces a firing squad.

Painting Number Thirteen

That we here highly resolve that these dead shall not have died in vain . . .

In this design Lincoln, as the champion of Federal Union, gives his message to our times and points to one world. With him stand Franklin Delano Roosevelt, Wilson, and Willkie, the great prophets and builders of the United Nations.

On the left, a widow and a bereaved family stand beneath a soldier crucified on the Cross of War.

In the right foreground lie the kid gloves, the high hat, the blackjack, and the pistol of outworn power diplomacy amid the ever-ready shells of the munitions makers. A bewhiskered and ancient diplomat of power politics sits tightly clutching the arms of the past.

Behind the diplomat, Harding scowls at the internationalists. Sitting beside him is Senator Lodge. At the feet of Lincoln, Mr. Stettinius looks forward at the New World. The figure holding the umbrella suggests Chamberlain and the appeasers. Behind him are the imperialists, the militarists, and the monopolists. To the left is Winston Churchill.

On the peace table are seen the bread and wine of consecration to our ideals, and the torn treaties and mailed fist of the materialists: shall these dead have died in vain, or do we go forward with the courage of high resolve, to fulfill the meaning of Lincoln's words?

Painting Number Fourteen

That this nation under God shall have a new birth of freedom . . .

This design portrays the rainbow of promise rising again over our nation's future. On the right the planners, the builders, the scientists, and the educators are working for America's vast new destiny.

On the left, happy people rejoice in the security of permanent World Peace with justice for all.

Painting Number Fifteen

. . . and that govemnent of the people,
by the people, for the people, shall
not perish from this earth.

Here appears the most forceful message of the Address. It presents the ideal that the peoples of the earth—north, south, east, and west—clasp hands in good will, in understanding, and in sanity. All races, colors, and creeds reach out toward each other in the will to live together in one world at peace, with justice and liberty everywhere.

Lincoln's Gettysburg Address is today the voice of America, of democracy, of the people rededicating our nation to her high destiny.